Persepolis

Vegetarian Recipes from Persia and Beyond

Sally Butcher

Interlink Books

An imprint of Interlink Publishing Group, Inc.
Northampton, Massachusetts

*For my Center Parcs BFFs: Lisette,
Kate, Jan, Fiona, Cathy, and Caroline.
Once a year is so not enough.*

Contents

Introduction 06

From the Bakery: Bread and Savory Pastries 10

Breaking Fast 36

Light Bites and Snacks 58

Cold Appetizers, Mezze, and Salads 84

Soup and Other Hot Appetizers 110

Main Courses I: Grains and Beans 136

Main Courses II: Bakes and Casseroles 160

Pickles and Preserves 182

Desserts and Sweet Treats 202

Drinks, Hot and Cold 230

Index 250
Acknowledgments 255

Introduction

To boldly go where no eggplant has gone before…

In this book I will take you to the Veggieverse: a whole planet (if not actual galaxy—yet) of marvelous meat-free food. It is of course an imaginary culinary federation rather than an actual must-visit intergalactic destination, but visit it we will…

When my book *The New Middle Eastern Vegetarian: Modern Recipes from Veggiestan* came out in 2012, a lot of people casually wondered where this brave new nation was. I became adept at straight-facedly telling them that it was just to the right of Kyrgyzstan, a tad to the left of Pakistan, and just above Snackistan. In truth **of** course, it is an entirely fictitious entity comprising the kitchens of the Middle East, minus the meaty fishy parts. A collation of vegetarian delights gathered from the lands stretching east from Morocco, meandering through Egypt and down as far as Somalia, and then up through the Levant and Turkey, across Central Asia, and down into Arabia.

Two things happened when I finished writing it. Firstly, I had so much material that swathes of it got left behind (some of which are gathered on my Veggiestan website). And secondly, I managed to convince myself that it was actually a real and viable state. When we decided, Mr. Shopkeeper and I, to broaden the remit of our Persian food business in Peckham, London and throw in a couple of random tables so we could feed hungry shoppers, it seemed only natural to breathe life into Veggiestan and make it a real republic—a landlocked café within the borders of Persepolis, the shop we have run together for nigh-on 16 years.

Mr. Shopkeeper was quite sceptical: who would want to come and eat, sandwiched between the shelves of a corner store? So we trod carefully, let the restaurant grow itself, one table at a time. But much to his surprise, people came and soon there were lines at the weekend. At least two tables got bashed together out of pallets and desperation (so don't be surprised if you visit and your table wobbles somewhat). Now we have 9½ tables, and Mr. S. has his eyes on the basement. Anyway, Persepolis has become a go-to destination for those looking for something meat-free and different, and so it seemed only natural to make this the book of the café of the shop* of the T-shirt of the same name. If you see what we mean…

Bizarrely, the UK government was one of the deciding factors in the writing of *Persepolis*. Not that it actually issued an edict or anything. It went and announced that we all need to eat "seven a day" (fruit and veggies, that is). Sales for the book enjoyed a little fillip overnight, our store was filled with people asking for vegetable help, and several journalists contacted us asking for veggie "sound bites."

The fact is that the part-time vegetarian who was identified in the book has become a thing—a whole legion of things. Great swathes of the population are now eschewing meat for the best part of the week in favor of healthier, vegetable-based alternatives. The appetite for new ways to brighten your broccoli, add sparkle to your spinach, and titillate

* the original book of the shop, *Persia in Peckham*, is still very much in print, but focuses uniquely on Persian food, meat and all.

PERSEPOLIS ²⁸
...FOR A TASTE OF PERSIA

your tomatillos has never been greater. We are collectively realizing, to quote an ancient Mesopotamian saying, that "He that takes medicine and neglects diet, wastes the skills of the physician."

I have been very lucky in the sense that the café has become my test kitchen, and my customers are now very much my guinea (soy alternative to) pigs. So I get constant feedback. There is no greater endorsement of a recipe than the sight of an empty plate coming back from the table. Previously, I relied mostly on my long-suffering, but carnivorous, beloved husband for second opinions.

In this vegetable-star-studded sequel, I venture a little further from the Middle Eastern shores, deserts, and mountain ranges to other continents and beyond... The book still mostly draws on my experience in Mediterranean and Middle Eastern cuisine, but once again I have nagged my customers from all parts of the globe to share their recipes (and stories).

Like all sequels, this is meant to be a stand-alone book. You do not need any working knowledge of my first volume to understand the thrilling plot twists and complex characters to be found on the following pages, nor have we graduated from beginner to intermediate: hopefully the recipes are just as simple and just as much fun. And once again I have, to a large extent, avoided tofu as a substitute for meat: my ethos is all about bigging up the vegetable rather than bemoaning the lack of meat and trying to replace it in food.

This book really is a celebration of the vegetable. Although John Evelyn (the famous seventeenth-century gardener and vegetarian pioneer) was not remotely Veggiestani, I have given him the freedom of the land: his paean to the vegetable (and vehement criticism of the eaters of "shambles" as he called meat) is as eloquent as it gets:

To this might we add that transporting consideration, becoming both our veneration and admiration of the infinitely wise and glorious author of nature, who has given to plants such astonishing properties; such fiery heat in some to warm and cherish, such coolness in others to temper and refresh, such pinguid juice to nourish and feed the body, such quickening acids to compel the appetite, and grateful vehicles to court the obedience of the palate, such vigour to renew and support our natural strength, such ravishing flavour and perfumes to recreate and delight us; in short, such spirituous and active force to animate and revive every faculty and part, to all the kinds of human, and, I had almost said heavenly capacity.

What shall we add more? Our Gardens present us with them all; and whilst the Shambles are covered with gore and stench, our Sallets escape the Insults of the summer-fly, purify and warm the blood against winter rage. Nor wants there variety in more abundance, than any of the former ages could shew.

And finally... Why did we call our shop Persepolis? Well, yes, there are several other thingamajigs of the same name. A 2,500-year-old palace/pleasure dome, aka Iran's most famous monument/tourist attraction, for one. And then there is the breathtakingly incisive comic book/movie by Marjane Sartrapi (Mr. S. swears that this is the story of his childhood too). And there is a very popular soccer team too. Persepolis is actually a Greek word, meaning "city of the Persians," and it was adopted during the conquests/antics of Alexander the Great. In Farsi, the ancient citadel is actually known as Takht-e-Jamshid, or Jamshid's Throne, because it is (was) believed that the ancient warrior/priest/king Jamshid founded it (and ruled there for a rumored 700 years). As Mr. Shopkeeper's name is Jamshid, and he is the undisputed king of this café/restaurant/shop, it seemed only natural to name our domain accordingly... So now you know.

1

from the Bakery

BREAD AND SAVORY PASTRIES